Colonial People

~ A ~
Slave Family

Bobbie Kalman & Amanda Bishop

✿ Crabtree Publishing Company

www.crabtreebooks.com

Created by Bobbie Kalman

Dedicated by Amanda Bishop
For my parents, who overwhelm me with their love, wisdom, and support

Editor-in-Chief
Bobbie Kalman

Editorial director
Niki Walker

Writing team
Bobbie Kalman
Amanda Bishop

Editor
Kathryn Smithyman

Copy editors
Molly Aloian
Rebecca Sjonger

Art director
Robert MacGregor

Design
Margaret Amy Reiach
Kymberly McKee Murphy

Production coordinator
Heather Fitzpatrick

Photo researchers
Laura Hysert
Jaimie Nathan

Consultant
Larry Watson, Ph.D.,
Department of History, Benedict College

Photographs and reproductions
Colonial Williamsburg Foundation: front cover, pages 3, 4, 5, 11, 13, 14,
    15, 16, 19, 21, 22, 23, 24, 25, 26, 27, 29, 31
The Metropolitan Museum of Art, Gift of Erving and Joyce Wolf, 1982.
    (1982.443.3) Photograph © 1982 The Metropolitan Museum of Art:
    page 30. Detail.
A Moment on Mulberry Row, by Nathanial K. Gibbs.
    Monticello/Thomas Jefferson Foundation, Inc.: page 1

Illustrations
Barbara Bedell: border on cover and all pages, back cover, pages 6, 7,
    8 (top), 9 (bottom), 15 (top), 20, 28 (middle)
Antoinette "Cookie" Bortolon: page 10
Margaret Amy Reiach: pages 8 (bottom), 9 (top), 12, 15 (bottom),
    17, 18, 24, 26, 28 (top, bottom)
Tiffany Wybouw: page 19

Digital prepress
Embassy Graphics

Printer
Worzalla Publishing Company

Crabtree Publishing Company

www.crabtreebooks.com   1-800-387-7650

PMB 16A	612 Welland Avenue	73 Lime Walk
350 Fifth Avenue	St. Catharines	Headington
Suite 3308	Ontario	Oxford
New York, NY	Canada	OX3 7AD
10118	L2M 5V6	United Kingdom

Cataloging-in-Publication Data
Kalman, Bobbie
    A slave family/Bobbie Kalman & Amanda Bishop.
        p. cm. -- (The colonial people series)
Includes index.
Introduces the personal relationships and daily activities that were
part of the family life of slaves in colonial America.
    ISBN 0-7787-0746-6 (RLB) -- ISBN 0-7787-0792-X (pbk.)
1. Slaves--United States--Social conditions--Juvenile literature.
2. Slaves--United States--Social life and customs--Juvenile literature.
3. Plantation life--United States--History--Juvenile literature.
4. African American families--History--Juvenile literature.
5. African Americans--History--To 1863--Juvenile literature.
6. United States--History--Colonial period, ca. 1600-1775. [1. Slaves--
United States--Social conditions. 2. Slaves--United States--Social
life and customs. 3. Plantation life. 4. African American families--
History. 5. African Americans--History--To 1863. 6. United States--
History--Colonial period, ca. 1600-1775.] I. Bishop, Amanda.
II. Title.
    E443 .K35 2003
    973' .0496073--dc21

                                                                    LC 2002012053

Contents

Quasheba's family

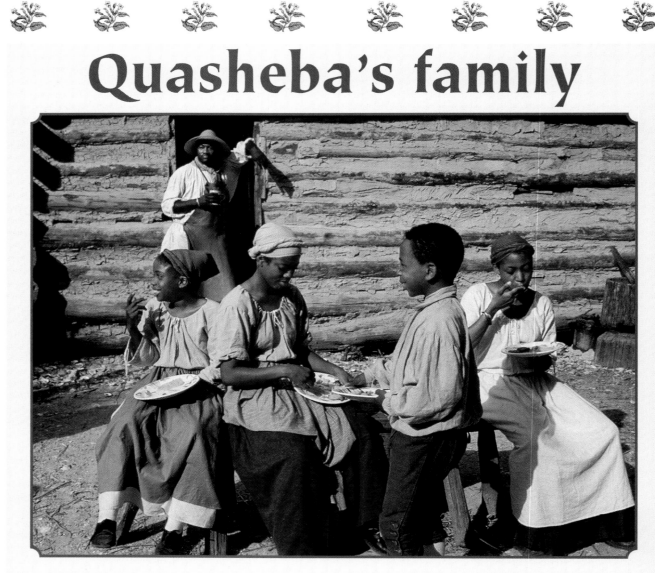

Quasheba awoke before daylight with a sinking feeling in her stomach. It was Saturday morning on the Johnstone **plantation**. Quasheba sat up and watched her mother and Aunt Jo preparing to leave for the field where they worked. Outside, some of the older men were laughing as they walked past the cabin in the **slave quarter**, but Quasheba did not feel like laughing. Noticing her long face, Aunt Jo exclaimed, "I'm so glad it's Saturday! Only half a day of work. Did I ever tell you about—" Quasheba's mother cut her off. "Not now! You'll be late. Out you go!" Jo obediently ducked out the door. Quasheba knew that her mother was only trying to help. The last time Jo was late for work, the **overseer** yelled at her in front of everyone and tried to embarrass her with insults. If Jo was late again, she would be punished! "You, too, slowpokes," Quasheba's mother said to her and her younger brother, Cuffee.

Off to the nursery

Quasheba's mother quickly kissed her son and daughter before following Jo out the door. Quasheba led Cuffee out of the cabin toward the **nursery**, where an older slave named Lizzie kept an eye on the slave children. Only twelve of the children were too young to work on the plantation. They went to the nursery to be fed and cared for, but they also spent a lot of time during the day doing chores for their families or playing with the **master's** children.

Quasheba and her brother tell stories with another young slave child.

Her last Saturday

As they walked, Quasheba's sad feeling returned. This was her last Saturday living with her family. On Monday, she would move into the master's house and become his daughter Mercy's servant. Quasheba didn't care much for Mercy Johnstone. Mercy was not very friendly to the slaves, and Quasheba especially hated when Mercy called her "Mary," the name given to her by Mr. Johnstone.

"Father's coming home!"

"Quasheba?" Cuffee whispered. Quasheba was so deep in thought that she had forgotten her little brother was beside her. Cuffee looked very excited. "Father's coming home today."

Quasheba watches Lizzie prepare a meal for the children in the nursery area.

Working in town

Quasheba smiled in spite of her sad mood. Her father was coming to visit. He worked as a blacksmith in town and came to see his family only when he could be spared from work.

Scary thoughts

The morning passed quickly as the children played games and jumped rope. They told scary stories about ghosts in the nearby woods, but Quasheba's thoughts were much scarier than any ghost story! After the weekend, she would no longer spend her days playing with her friends or have her mother kiss her good night.

A family afternoon

When Quasheba and Cuffee returned to their cabin in the afternoon, their mother was already back from the fields and working in the family's tiny garden. They joined her and started picking some black-eyed peas for supper. Soon Aunt Jo came along, singing a happy song. Cuffee and his mother joined her, but Quasheba didn't feel much like singing. The happy sounds made her feel even more upset.

Quasheba's father is a skilled blacksmith who has been hired out to work in a shop in town. He learned his skills in the plantation blacksmith shop.

A chance for an easier life

Before long, night fell. The slave quarter buzzed with songs and laughter, but Quasheba and her family stayed in their cabin. They wanted to be home when Father arrived. The hours passed, and both Aunt Jo and Cuffee fell asleep. Quasheba stared into the fire, thinking about her new life. Tears began to roll down her face. Finally, her mother said to her in a quiet voice, "I know you don't want to go, child. But you are very lucky to be moving to Mr. Johnstone's house. Your life will be much easier than mine has been." Before Quasheba could respond, she heard the sound of heavy footsteps outside the cabin.

Proud of Quasheba

"Anybody home?" a deep voice called. Cuffee's eyes opened at the sound of his father's voice. He squealed with delight and ran to throw his arms around his father. Soon everyone was hugging and kissing. Quasheba's father held her close and whispered, "I hear my girl is proper enough to live in Mr. Johnstone's house. I'm so proud of you, Quasheba. You'll do your job well, and Gran will be there in the kitchen if you need her." Quasheba beamed at the mention of her grandmother, after whom she was named. With her Gran nearby, she would not feel so alone. Her life among strangers may hold some hope, after all.

Perhaps Quasheba will be able to spend time in the kitchen, where Gran works. Maybe Cuffee can visit her. Do you think these things will happen? Read the rest of the book and finish Quasheba's story yourself. Will you give it a happy ending?

Slavery in the colonies

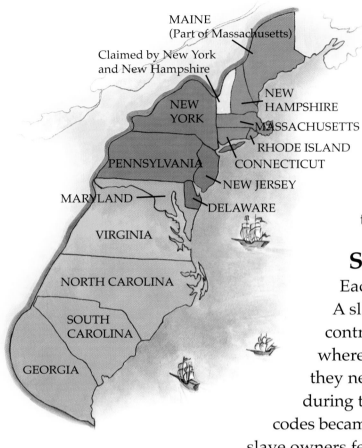

MAINE
(Part of Massachusetts)

Claimed by New York
and New Hampshire

NEW
YORK

NEW
HAMPSHIRE

MASSACHUSETTS

RHODE ISLAND

PENNSYLVANIA

CONNECTICUT

NEW JERSEY

MARYLAND

DELAWARE

VIRGINIA

NORTH CAROLINA

SOUTH
CAROLINA

GEORGIA

Quasheba's story is set in the **colony** of Virginia, which was one of the colonies that became the United States. Like all slaves in **colonial** times, Quasheba and her family were forced to work without pay. Colonists began using slaves from Africa in the early 1600s. In time, many areas became dependent on slave workers, and slaves soon outnumbered the European colonists.

Slavery laws

Each colony had its own **slavery code**. A slavery code was made up of laws that controlled the activities of slaves, such as where slaves could go and whose permission they needed. Slavery codes changed many times during the colonial period. In some colonies, the codes became stricter as slave populations grew because slave owners feared that the slaves might **rebel**.

The southern colonies

The southern colonies—Maryland, Virginia, North Carolina, South Carolina, and Georgia—were most dependent on slave labor. Much of the business in these colonies was based on **cash crops**, or crops grown only to be sold, such as tobacco, rice, and **indigo**. The crops had to be planted, tended, and harvested by hand. Slavery did not become **legal** in the southern colonies until the late 1600s or early 1700s, but most used slave labor long before it was legal to do so. In 1750, Georgia became the last colony to legalize slavery. Slave codes in the South were very strict, and slaves were often treated poorly.

The middle colonies

The middle colonies included New York, New Jersey, Pennsylvania, and Delaware. In these colonies, slaves worked as **field hands**, **house servants** (right), and **tradespeople** such as miners, millers, tanners, and coopers. New York and New Jersey quickly passed laws to stop slaves from becoming skilled tradespeople, but slaves continued to work in the trades as laborers. In Pennsylvania, slaves were used from about 1700. Most worked on farms in the southern part of the colony, but some also worked for tradespeople in the cities. The slavery codes were strict, but the treatment of slaves in most of the middle colonies was slightly better than it was in the southern colonies. There were few slaves in Delaware, but they were treated in much the same way as the slaves were in the southern colonies.

The northern colonies

Slavery in the northern colonies—New Hampshire, Massachusetts, Rhode Island, and Connecticut—was very different from slavery in the South. In Rhode Island, dairy farmers used slaves to maintain farms and help tend livestock. In the other northern colonies, together called New England, slaves lived in towns or cities along the coast. They worked as servants and tradespeople such as coopers, woodworkers, and smiths. Many New England slave owners practiced **family slavery**. They purchased young slave children, whom they raised as part of their families. They educated the young slaves and trained them to work in family businesses. The practice of "adopting" slave children meant that many slave families were torn apart.

This tradesman is a shinglemaker.

Slave families

The story of Quasheba's family is not true, but it is based on the lives of slaves in colonial times. The grandparents and great-grandparents of girls like Quasheba were kidnapped from Africa, brought to the New World, and sold as slaves. Their children and grandchildren were born into slavery.

Split apart

Slaves were bought, sold, and traded by colonists as if they were objects. Many slaves were purchased at **slave auctions**. At a slave auction, a slave was sold to the colonist that offered the most money. Slave families were often split up at auctions so that members could be sold individually. Family members were often sold to different owners, who gave the slaves new European names.

Making a profit

Once slaves arrived at their owners' homes, they were expected to do many different kinds of work. Some were cooks or servants in the homes of wealthy masters. Others worked on farms or in workshops. Since slaves were not paid for their work, many slave owners became wealthy by selling the products of slave labor.

Few rights

Slaves did not have the same rights that European colonists had. They were not recognized as people by the laws of the colonies, so they were not able to make legal contracts. Without the right to make contracts, slaves could not marry.

Allowing families

Some owners allowed and even encouraged their slaves to marry and start families, however, because the children of the slaves became their property as well. Many owners also believed that slaves with families were less likely to cause trouble because they feared being sold and sent away from their loved ones.

Breaking ties

Slave families lived with the constant fear of having family members sold or hired out to owners who lived far away. As "property," slaves could be bought or sold at any time without warning and without their consent. Some masters tried not to break up families, but most gave little thought to the wishes of the slaves. Some colonists even believed that the feelings of slaves were different from their own. They did not think slaves would be heartbroken if they were separated from their families.

Love and support

For slaves, the love and support of family and
friends helped make life bearable. They enjoyed
the little free time they had together by chatting,
singing, and playing games. When a loved one
was sold or sent away to work, family members
stayed in touch by sending messages through
slaves who traveled with their masters.

Marriage and children

Slave marriages were not recognized by the law and were always in danger of being broken by owners, but slaves married nevertheless. Some slaves got married without ceremonies. Others had weddings, during which they exchanged marriage vows in front of their friends and families. Respected older slaves usually performed the ceremonies. In some cases, ministers or slave owners performed them. As part of their wedding ceremonies, many slaves practiced a ritual called "jumping the broom," which is shown above. The ritual had different meanings to different people. Some people believed that jumping across the broom meant making the leap into married life. Others jumped backwards over the broom and joked that the person who jumped the farthest would have the upper hand in the marriage.

Having children

Pregnant slave women continued to work at their jobs until shortly before they gave birth. Some masters allowed pregnant slaves to stop working for two months—one before giving birth and one afterward. Other slave owners forced pregnant women to keep working until they gave birth and reduced their workload only during the last month. Babies were delivered by slave **midwives**, but the wives of owners were sometimes present to help.

Naming the baby

Just as Quasheba was named after her grandmother, slave parents often gave their babies the same names as those of their relatives. Many also followed naming customs from Africa, such as naming babies according to their birth order or the days of the week on which they were born. According to some naming practices, a girl born on a Monday was called Juba, and a boy born on a Friday was called Cuffee.

Secret names

Some owners insisted on naming slave babies, just as they renamed any older slaves they purchased. The slaves had no choice but to allow their babies to be renamed by their owners. Secretly, though, they called the babies by their original names. Slaves used these names when the slave owners could not hear them.

A wedding was a happy occasion because it meant the beginning of a new life for both the husband and wife.

13

Helping one another

Slave families who were able to live together did their best to make good homes for themselves. Each member of the family contributed to the household in his or her own way. Everyone shared chores and responsibilities to make life easier. Some fathers, uncles, and sons used their spare moments to carve wooden bowls, spoons, and other utensils for their homes. They built beds, tables, chairs, and benches out of scrap wood or trees from nearby forests. Mothers, aunts, and older daughters stuffed mattresses with straw or corn husks and sewed fabric scraps into quilts.

(left) Women were more likely than men to stay in one place all their lives. Mothers, aunts, sisters, and other female relatives kept family ties strong.

All family members helped tend their tiny gardens. The vegetables they grew made their small meals more healthy and filling.

14

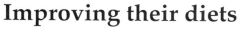

Improving their diets

Slave owners provided food for their slaves, but the portions were small and not very nutritious. If their owners allowed it, families kept gardens near their cabins. They grew vegetables  and herbs to add to their meals. Children helped weed the gardens and harvest the crops. Many fathers and older sons took time after a long day's work to hunt for small animals such as opossums, rabbits, and squirrels. Slaves who lived near ponds, lakes, and streams could also fish and catch turtles. Some slaves even made canoes from hollowed logs and used them for fishing trips. Slaves who lived near oceans added clams, oysters, crabs, and shrimps to their diets.

The rabbit this man trapped will add more meat to the family meal.

Family elders

Grandparents, great aunts and uncles, and other elderly adults did their best to help raise the children. They sang songs, told tales and riddles, and shared the knowledge and memories of their lives before slavery. Older family members also helped with the cooking, gardening, and fishing whenever they could. The most important responsibility of the elderly slaves, however, was to keep peace in the quarter. Elder slaves were greatly respected. Family members turned to them for help and advice in decision-making.

Learning by listening

Children were expected to respect and obey all the adult slaves in the quarter. The adults shared the responsibility of raising and entertaining the children, whether they were relatives or not.

The lives of slave children

In the story, Quasheba's brother, Cuffee, was too young to work for the master, but Quasheba was about to start her life as a house servant. Slave owners rarely expected children to work before the age of ten. Until that age, children were free to do as they pleased with little supervision. Most slave children spent their days doing chores for their families or playing with one another and the children of their owners. The children of slave owners sometimes became close friends and strong allies of slave children. They could sneak extra food for slave children, protect them from punishment, and even try to keep them from being sold. When slave children became their servants, however, their attitudes often changed and old friendships were forgotten.

Play time
Slave children played many games to pass their free time. They ran through forests and meadows, played **hoops**, jumped rope, traded marbles, and went fishing. They also made games out of events they witnessed but did not understand, such as slave auctions and punishments.

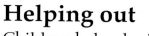

Looking after one another

Some plantations had nurseries where slave children went while their parents worked. An older female slave, called a **nurse**, fed and cared for the children under the supervision of the slave owner's wife. When there was no nursery, children often had to care for their younger siblings. An elderly slave in the quarter usually looked out for the young "nurses" and made sure that they were taking proper care of the children. The time slave children spent together gave them a chance to strengthen their bonds with younger brothers and sisters.

Helping out

Children helped with their family's workload whenever they could. They pulled weeds and watered the vegetable garden so their parents did not have to do these extra chores after a long day's work. Children also learned to hunt and trap small animals to add to the family meals. As they grew older, they were sometimes given small jobs to do for their owners. They chased pests out of the yards and fields, acted as messengers, did small chores for the kitchen staff, and brought water to the slaves working in the fields.

Leaving home

In New England, slave children were often taken from their own families and brought to live with the families of slave owners. They were raised as members of the owners' families and were not allowed to visit their parents. Phillis Wheatley, America's first African poet, was a family slave. Her first book of poetry was published in 1773.

The education of slaves

Going to school

Most slave children never had a formal education. For a short time, however, the Bray School in Williamsburg, Virginia, and Elias Neau's school in New York were permitted to teach slave children to read and write. A slave named Newport Gardner, who was allowed to take music lessons, was so talented that he opened his own school of music in Rhode Island for slaves and non-slaves alike.

Few slaves were allowed to attend school. Time spent at school meant time away from their jobs, and slaves were valuable to their owners only when they worked. Since slaves usually worked in the fields or in their masters' homes (see pages 22-25), most colonists did not feel that slaves needed a formal education. Many colonists also feared that slaves who knew how to read and write might spread messages and convince one another to rebel against their owners.

The lucky few

Some owners chose to teach their slaves to read, write, and do arithmetic because they believed an education made slaves more valuable. Educated slaves, in turn, taught their skills to other slaves. Slave children were occasionally allowed to sit in on lessons given to a slave owner's children. Most slaves had to be taught secretly, however, as it soon became illegal to educate them. Sometimes a slave owner's children taught the slaves to read and write, even though they were not allowed to.

18

Life skills

Most slave children were educated by their family members and other adult slaves in the quarter.  They helped the adults with chores and in the process learned sewing, weaving, cooking, and hunting skills. Working together helped make chores more enjoyable, and it helped prepare children for adulthood.

Learning "slave" behavior

Parents and older slaves also taught skills that were important to the children's well-being around slave owners. By watching adults, slave children learned how to behave in order to avoid punishment. They saw which words and actions pleased masters and which ones made them angry. Children also learned to stay quiet at an early age so they would not say things that might get their families in trouble. Some owners tricked young slaves into spying on their families or other slaves in the quarter.

Telling stories

Slave children also learned many important lessons through stories and folktales. Parents and elder members of the slave community shared stories with the children to teach them **values** and **morals**. For more on these stories, see page 28.

Slaves taught their children special skills such as cooking or basket-weaving, as shown above. If the skills were useful to the owner, he or she was less likely to sell or hire out the children.

Life on a plantation

Quasheba's family lived and worked on a plantation. Most slaves on a plantation lived in a slave quarter, which was located away from the master's house and near the fields. Not all plantations were the same size. Some were very small with only a few slaves. In later years, many plantations were huge and had hundreds of slaves.

The large home in the picture below is the master's house. Beside it is the kitchen, which often housed the slaves who did the cooking. Other buildings on the plantation included the barn, laundry, spring house, and ice house. Some plantations also had workshops such as a blacksmith's shop and a carpentry shop.

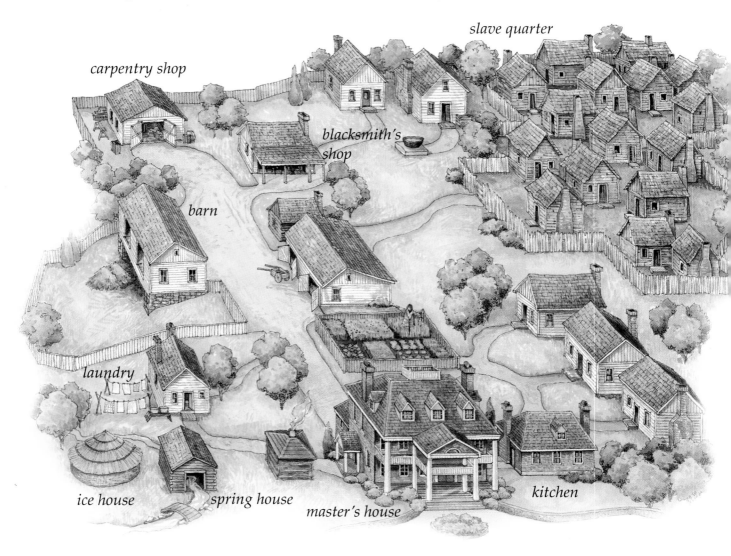

A plantation of this size was home to up to 40 slaves.

The planter's family

Unmarried women and widows could own slaves, but most slave owners were men. The **planter**, or plantation owner, managed the money and farm work on the plantation and controlled the activities of slaves. The **mistress**, or planter's wife, ran her household. She directed the house servants on how to prepare meals and look after her children.

Field work

It took a lot of work to keep a plantation running. Slaves did the hardest and most unpleasant jobs, while the planter and his family enjoyed the rewards. Since the planter made money by selling crops, most of the work on a plantation was farm work. Field hands outnumbered other types of slaves on most plantations.

Work in the master's house

House servants did the chores that kept the planter's home running. Quasheba was about to become a servant to her owner's daughter, Mercy. Quasheba's grandmother was a cook who worked in the kitchen house, preparing meals for Mr. Johnstone's family and guests.

The craft shops

Many plantations had workshops where skilled slaves, such as Quasheba's father, made wooden and metal items needed for the farm and the planter's household. The planter made money by selling extra items and hiring out skilled slaves.

Finding time together

Most slaves had little free time to spend with their families. They worked from ten to twelve hours a day, six days a week. Family members who lived on the same plantation had just an hour or two together before they went to bed at the end of a long day. Some husbands and wives lived on different plantations, however, so they did not even see each other every day. Family members could visit each other only on Sundays and holidays—and only if their owners allowed it. In spite of the difficulties, slave families and friends made a great effort to find time for one another.

Field hands

Quasheba's mother and aunt were field hands. Field hands worked tilling the soil, planting and harvesting crops, tending the livestock, and looking after the master's property. Field work was very demanding. Slaves had to work from just after sunrise until very late in the day, with only a short meal break. The labor was exhausting, but field hands were not allowed to rest or stop working, even for a few moments.

An overseer made sure that everyone kept working hard all day long. The owner, a hired man, or a trusted slave acted as the overseer. He punished any slaves he caught pausing or even slowing down. Punishments could be severe. They sometimes involved **whippings**, during which a slave was tied to a tree or a whipping post and lashed many times on the back with a strip of leather.

The overseer (far left) had a difficult job if he was a slave. If he was hard on the other slaves, he became an outcast. If he was easy on the slaves, the slave owner punished or replaced him.

Staying in line

No slave wanted to be punished, so field hands were careful to do exactly what was expected of them whenever the overseer was nearby. Overseers often punished slaves in front of others to make examples of them. It was especially hard for family members to watch a loved one being whipped because they could do nothing to stop it.

House servants

This house servant lays out clothes for her mistress every morning.

House servants lived and worked in the homes of slave owners. Many house servants began to work at an early age. They had to leave their families in the quarter to do so, just as Quasheba was about to leave hers. In towns and cities, house servants were often sent to work for other owners and had to leave their families altogether.

Household duties

House servants did all kinds of chores. They were responsible for cooking, cleaning, spinning, weaving, sewing, gardening, going to market, running errands, and waiting on their masters' families and guests. Some house servants worked full-time for only one member of a family.

House servants often cared for their masters' children and developed special bonds with them.

Life in the house

House servants were either very young, like Quasheba, or quite old—especially on plantations. Many planters believed that strong, healthy adult slaves were better used in fields and workshops. House servants did not always have their own rooms inside the house. Many slept on **pallets**, or mats, on the stairs or in the bedrooms of their owners. The slaves could be called at any time, day or night, and had to answer quickly whenever their owners needed them. House slaves were often mistreated because they were close at hand when their masters' tempers flared.

A different lifestyle

House servants usually had better food and clothing than field hands had. They were given leftover food from meals and received old clothes from their masters' families. House servants were much closer to their owners than other slaves were. Many owners took no notice of their servants, so they spoke and acted freely in front of these slaves. House servants learned to be careful not to show their owners that they noticed these private conversations or actions, and they rarely repeated their owners' secrets. Quasheba would have to learn to say the right things when she became a servant!

Tradespeople

Some slaves, such as Quasheba's father, were trained as blacksmiths, house builders, carpenters, wheelwrights, cabinetmakers, tanners, shoemakers, coopers, or wigmakers. Slave owners valued skilled slaves because their work brought in extra income. The slaves could be hired out to tradespeople to work in shops or at building sites. Although becoming skilled workers often meant time away from their homes and families, most slaves were happy to be given opportunities to learn new skills. Having skills gave them a chance to earn extra money in their spare time. With this money, a slave could buy things that his or her family needed,

such as cooking utensils, fabric, or new clothing. In the northern colonies, many European tradespeople complained because so much work was given to skilled slaves that the tradespeople could not find jobs. These colonies soon passed laws that limited the use of skilled slaves. As a result, nothern slaves could work only as laborers.

It was never too early to start learning a skill such as working with wood. Quasheba's uncle and another woodworker show Cuffee and his young friend how to saw a log. The wood will be used in the cabinetmaker's shop.

Going home

Slaves did not have to work on Sundays, so Saturday nights and Sundays were the only times that a hired-out slave could see his family. He often walked several miles on a Saturday night to return to his home for a visit. He had to get permission before making the trip, however. Some renters refused to allow their hired slaves to leave their properties. Many slaves were so anxious to see their families that they sneaked away despite the threat of being caught and punished.

Wigmaking was a valuable trade in the colonies, where many wealthy men wore wigs in public.

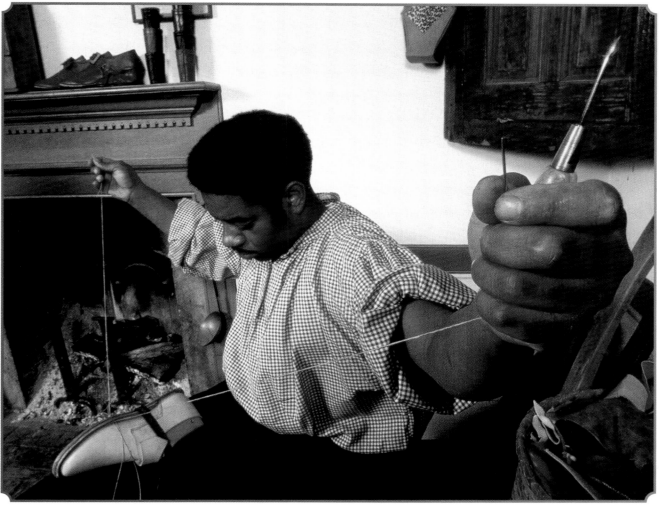

This slave's skills as a shoemaker allow him to make some extra money for his family. He is treated well by his master because of his abilities.

Culture from Africa

In early colonial times, most slaves were Africans who were brought to the colonies by force. They had strong cultural backgrounds and fond memories of their lives as free people in Africa. They held on to their cultures and identities when they could and passed them on to later **generations** of slaves who were born in the colonies. The older slaves in a community were often responsible for sharing African culture. They recited stories and fables to the children about talking animals and spirits. These tales taught important lessons about behavior and survival.

Looks like home

Many slaves fashioned objects that reminded them of Africa. They taught their children how to make baskets and rugs in African styles. Slaves also made musical instruments similar to those used in Africa. One such instrument was a shaker, shown right, which was made from a dried gourd covered with a netting of homemade beads. Another was a three-stringed instrument that was similar to a banjo.

Drumming

Slaves made drums by stretching animal skins over bases of hollowed wood. They danced to the beat of the drums. They also made up codes and sent one another messages using drumbeats. When suspicious owners took away the drums, slaves simply drummed on their bodies and tapped their feet instead.

Special songs

Slaves sang songs in a **call-and-response pattern**, in which listeners answered the singer, as they had in Africa. Everyone could take part in these songs. Slaves sang during work, while celebrating, and to communicate secret messages.

Food and recipes

Foods such as peanuts, yams, and sesame seeds, or "benne," gave slaves a small taste of Africa. Slaves not only used African foods when cooking for themselves, but they introduced new dishes to the colonists as well. Many slaves also knew some traditional **folk medicine**. They made potions and **poultices** to treat illnesses and relieve pain.

Time for fun

At special gatherings, such as the one shown below, slaves sang, danced, laughed, and told stories by a fire until late into the night. Celebrations gave slaves a chance to enjoy the music, dancing, folklore, and foods of their heritage. Husbands and wives were happy to spend some time together, and children enjoyed singing and dancing.

Some owners allowed their slaves to hold such gatherings in the quarters. Dances were held, and slaves from miles around attended. The gatherings were a chance for people to catch up with friends and relatives whom they did not see very often. In many areas, however, slaves had to meet in secret because it was against the law for them to gather without an owner's supervision.

The cost of freedom

Many colonial slaves were born into slavery and never knew freedom, but some were **manumitted**, or freed, by their owners. Still others were able to buy their freedom with money they saved up over time. If a skilled slave had enough money, he could buy freedom for himself and purchase it for his family members as well.

extra work to make money with which to buy his or her freedom. Some slaves were freed by the governments of their colonies for providing a great service. For instance, in Virginia and South Carolina, two slaves who were famous healers were freed because their natural remedies for illnesses and snake bites helped save the lives of many colonists.

Chances for freedom

In the early colonial period, slaves had a better chance of being freed than slaves later on had. A slave might earn freedom by working for many years or by doing

Afraid of slaves

As more slaves were brought to the colonies, slave owners grew concerned about the influence of freed slaves. Some colonists were afraid that freed slaves

might encourage other slaves to fight for their freedom. The colonies passed laws that made it increasingly difficult for owners to manumit their slaves. At one time, slave owners could sell their slaves freedom or allow them to be freed after the owners died. Before long, however, slave owners had to get permission from the government to free slaves. They often had to pay a fee to the government to do so.

Those who got away

In late colonial New England, slaves could sue their owners for their freedom. If slaves had done exceptional work, the court sometimes allowed them to go free.

Former slaves were somewhat restricted even after they were freed, but they were no longer seen as property. They could live on their own and, if they earned enough money, purchase freedom for their loved ones.

Making a break

In most colonies, slaves who became fed up with their lives had no choice but to run away. Few runaways were successful because slave owners went to great lengths to recapture them. Some runaway slaves formed small villages in remote wild areas. As soon as slave owners discovered the secret villages, however, they destroyed them.

What happened to Quasheba?

As you have seen, any number of things could have happened to Quasheba and her family. Mercy Johnstone may have married, moved away, and taken Quasheba with her. Cuffee may have come to work in the master's house as a servant, or his father may have taught him how to be a blacksmith. Together, Cuffee and his father may have earned enough money blacksmithing to purchase their freedom, as well as that of the rest of the family. Maybe one night, when Quasheba's father was home, Quasheba was able to sneak away from the master's house, and the family ran away together. Perhaps the whole family was freed after Mr. Johnstone died. What ending would you give to the story of Quasheba and her family?

Glossary

Note: Boldfaced words that are defined in the book may not appear in the glossary.

colonial Relating to living in a colony or to a period when European countries ruled North America

colony An area ruled by a faraway country, such as England or France

colonist A person who lived in a colony

field hand A slave who worked in the fields of a farm or plantation

folk medicine Traditional ways of using natural ingredients to heal

generation A group of people who are born and live at about the same time

house servant A slave who lived and worked in the home of his or her owner

hoops A game in which one person rolls a hoop in a straight line and another person tries to throw a stick through the hoop as it rolls past

indigo A plant used to make blue dye

legal Describing an action that is allowed by law

master A slave owner

midwife A woman who is trained to help women give birth

moral An idea about which behavior is right and which is wrong

nursery An area on a plantation that was set aside for slave children

overseer One who kept watch over the work of slaves

plantation A large farm with a main crop

poultice A natural treatment for infection

rebel To oppose or resist, often with force

slave quarter On a plantation, an area near the fields where slaves lived

tradesperson A person whose occupation requires special training or skill

value An idea considered to be important

Index

1 2 3 4 5 6 7 8 9 0 Printed in the U.S.A. 2 1 0 9 8 7 6 5 4 3